HOW TO IMPROVE AT KARATE

All the information you need to know
to get on top of your game!

More than just instructional guides, the **HOW TO IMPROVE AT...**
series gives you everything you need to achieve your goals—tips on
technique, step-by-step demonstrations, nutritional advice, and the secrets
of successful pro athletes. Excellent visual instructions and expert advice
combine to act as your own personal trainer. These books aim to give you
the know-how and confidence to improve your performance.

Studies have shown that an active approach to life makes you feel happier
and less stressed. The easiest way to start is by taking up a new sport or
improving your skills in an existing one. You simply have to choose an
activity that enthuses you.

HOW TO IMPROVE AT KARATE does not promise instant success.
It simply gives you the tools to become the best at whatever you choose
to do.

*Every care has been taken to ensure that these instructions are safe to follow, but in the
event of injury Crabtree Publishing shall not be liable for any injuries or damages.*

By Ashley Martin

Crabtree Publishing Company
www.crabtreebooks.com

Cover: Karate champion Luca Valdesi
With thanks to: Gareth Randall and Lizzie Knowles
ticktock project editors: Jo Hanks and Joe Harris
ticktock project designer: Sara Greasley
Photography: Kevin Wood of Scott–Wood Photography
Illustrations: Hayley Terry

Photo credits: Steve Bardens/ Action Plus: p. 46 right;
Bongarts/ Getty Images: p. 47 bottom; Getty Images:
p. 47 top; Getty Images for DAGOC: p. 46 left; iStock:
p. 6 top, p. 43 bottom; Jupiter Images: p. 6 bottom;
Photolibrary Group: p. 7 bottom, front cover; Pekka
Sakki/ Rex Features: p. 45 top left; Shutterstock: p. 7 top,
p. 44 top; Hayley Terry: p. 9; ticktock Media Archive:
p. 3 bottom.

Library and Archives Canada Cataloguing in Publication

Martin, Ashley P., 1972-
    How to improve at karate / Ashley Martin.

(How to improve at--)
Includes index.
ISBN 978-0-7787-3568-7 (bound).--ISBN 978-0-7787-3590-8 (pbk.)

    1. Karate--Training--Juvenile literature. I. Title. II. Series.

GV1114.3.M374 2007   j796.815'3   C2007-906483-3

Library of Congress Cataloging-in-Publication Data

Martin, Ashley.
    How to improve at karate / Ashley Martin.
        p. cm. -- (How to improve at)
    Includes index.
    ISBN-13: 978-0-7787-3568-7 (rlb)
    ISBN-10: 0-7787-3568-0 (rlb)
    ISBN-13: 978-0-7787-3590-8 (pb)
    ISBN-10: 0-7787-3590-7 (pb)
    1. Karate for children--Juvenile literature. I. Title. II. Series.

GV1114.32.M37 2007
796.815'3083--dc22
                                        2007043676

Crabtree Publishing Company
www.crabtreebooks.com   1-800-387-7650

Published in Canada
Crabtree Publishing
616 Welland Ave.
St. Catharines, Ontario
L2M 5V6

Published in the United States
Crabtree Publishing
PMB16A
350 Fifth Ave., Suite 3308
New York, NY 10118

CONTENTS

INTRODUCTION

Karate is an exciting sport and a traditional martial art with a fascinating history. Karate can be used for self defence, but it has many other benefits—it can improve health, build physical fitness, and boost your self-confidence. The word "karate" comes from two Japanese characters: kara, meaning "empty", and te, meaning "hand".

ELEMENTS OF KARATE

Karate training is split into three sections.

BASICS (*KIHON*)

These are the essential techniques that make up karate, including stances, punches, blocks and kicks. The kihon are found in the "karate techniques" section of this book.

FORMS (*KATA*)

Kata are traditional choreographed sequences of moves performed as if fighting a series of imaginary opponents. The kata contain the self defence techniques of karate. It takes years of training to fully understand the kata.

SPARRING (*KUMITE*)

The kumite section of karate involves sparring with a partner. At the beginner level, this is a set routine of punches and blocks. Some of these are covered in the "Skills and Drills" section of this book. At the highest level, kumite is a fighting contest.

ORIGINS OF KARATE

Karate was started in Okinawa, a small island found near China, which is today a part of Japan. The traditional elements of karate were developed in Okinawa but have a strong Chinese influence. Modern elements of karate—such as sports karate and the belt system—originated in Japan.

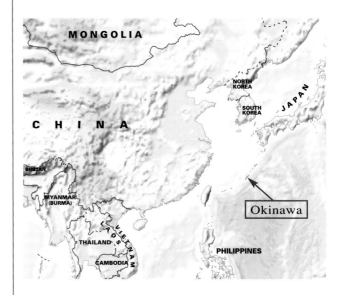

EQUIPMENT

*K*arate does not require a lot of equipment. There is a simple uniform with a variety of belt colors, which signify a person's skill level. In addition to the uniform, other equipment is used to keep everyone safe.

KARATE UNIFORM

The karate uniform is called a "*dogi*" in Japanese—often it is just called a "*gi*".
Usually, the uniform is made from white cotton. It does not have much decoration, except for a club badge on the left breast. The gi is held together with a belt. The color of the belt shows rank.

PUNCH BAGS

Punch bags and strike shields are used to practice powerful kicks and punches.
For best results, attack as if your target is actually a few inches behind the bag. That way, you put all of your power into the bag. Start slowly at first, then increase the power.

FOCUS PADS

Focus pads are used to improve your targeting and speed.
Practice hitting the target in the center. Some focus pads have target spots in the center for you to aim at.

CRASH MATS

It is usual to practice moves without any mats, because you want to stay on your feet in karate.
However, mats are often used in competition so that you don't get hurt if someone sweeps or throws you. You should always use mats if you are doing any exercises that involve throws or sweeps.

As karate students move from beginner to expert, their levels are shown with the colored-belt system.

The grades of the first ten belts are called "kyu". After that, there are ten grades of black belt, called "dan". Each belt requires you to perform specific skills in a grading examination. If you train hard enough, you will usually take an examination every three months. With regular training, most people can earn a black belt in three to five years.

White

Beginner

Orange

9th kyu – 3 months

Red

8th kyu – 6 months

Yellow

7th kyu – 9 months

Green

6th kyu – 1 year

Purple

5th kyu – 1 year & 3 months

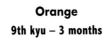

Purple and White

4th kyu – 1 year & 6 months

Brown

3rd kyu – 1 year & 9 months

Brown and White

2nd kyu – 2 years

Brown and 2 White Stripes

1st kyu – 2 years & 3 months

Black

1st dan – 3 years

HOW TO TIE YOUR BELT

There are several correct ways of tying a karate belt.
A properly tied belt is less likely to fall off during training. Tying your belt correctly takes only a little bit of practice.

Make sure that you adjust the belt so that both of the ends are the same length.

STEP 1

Pass the belt behind you and hold either end. Make sure that the belt is short on one side and long on the other.

STEP 3

Take the end that you wrapped around yourself, tuck it around the short end, and then up under the section that you are holding by your bellybutton.

STEP 2

Hold the short end closer to your middle, and wrap the longer end around your body once. Then hold the two ends together near your bellybutton.

STEP 4

Now tie a simple knot in the belt. Pull on both ends to tighten it.

PROTECTIVE EQUIPMENT

Protective equipment is rarely used in a karate class. Most sparring exercises are expected to be performed with control, so there is no danger of injury. However, some protective equipment must be used for serious sparring training or matches. Each competition has different rules about what protection should be used.

HEAD GUARDS

A standard head guard has padding for the sides of the head and the forehead. Some head guards also have a face grill. The grill protects against the head punches that are common in karate.

ARM PADS

Forearm padding can reduce the risk of bruising when blocking heavy attacks, or when being blocked.

SHIN GUARDS

Shin padding protects against bruising when legs clash together during a kick or a foot sweep.

GROIN GUARDS

A groin guard is essential for any sparring match.

MITTS

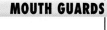

Karate mitts cover the knuckles and the backs of the hands. Some gloves also protect the wrists and parts of the forearms.

CHEST PROTECTION

For most karate matches, men wear no chest protection. Women can wear a hard plastic chest protector under their karate uniforms. In full-contact matches, both men and women wear padded vests over their chests.

MOUTH GUARDS

A mouth guard protects the teeth. If you are not wearing a head guard with a face grill, then this guard is needed for sparring. Most people use a "boil and bite" self-fitted mouth guard. You can also get a professionally fitted gum sheild.

FOOT GUARDS

Foot guards protect your feet when you are kicking during sparring matches.

THE KARATE DOJO

The dojo is any place where karate training takes place. Karate can be performed in almost any space, large or small—you can even practice outside in good weather. However, karate classes usually take place in a sports hall or custom-built dojo. It is important to behave properly inside the karate dojo.

MENTAL PREPARATION

It is common to bow when entering and leaving the dojo. *Bowing helps prepare the mind for training as you enter and clears the mind before leaving.*

PARTNER WORK

Karate students must show respect to their fellow students during sparring. They must control their attacks and stay the right distance from their partners to avoid injuries.

THE SENSEI

Karate classes are taught by an instructor with a black belt. The instructor is called "*sensei*", which is a Japanese word for teacher. *Pay attention to what your sensei tells you, especially about your safety. If you are late for a practice, wait for the instructor to tell you when you may join in.*

LINE WORK

Karate lessons start by lining up the students in belt-grade order. Each grade then performs movements according to their levels. *Karate classes can range from six to 100 students in a lesson. Students line up a safe distance apart to avoid hitting one another.*

DOJO ETIQUETTE

You will be expected to behave a certain way while you are in the dojo. Here are some specific rules:
- *Keep toenails and fingernails short.*
- *Do not wear jewellry or watches during training.*
- *Keep your training uniform clean and in good condition.*
- *Show respect to one another.*

THE COMPETITION AREA

*O*fficial karate competitions are held on a matted area, which is surrounded by safety mats. Usually, the competition area is green, and the safety area is red. Competitors must stay within the green area. If they move into the safety area, they are either given a warning or must forfeit points to their opponents.

KEY INSTRUCTIONS DURING A FIGHT

The referee's instructions are usually in Japanese. These are the most important:

Hajime
Start. You must wait for the referee to say "hajime" before you start fighting.

Yame
Stop. You must stop fighting immediately.

Chui
Warning. If you break any rules, you will hear this as a warning.

Jogai
If you step out of the green area the referee will shout "jogai".

THE COMPETITION SPACE

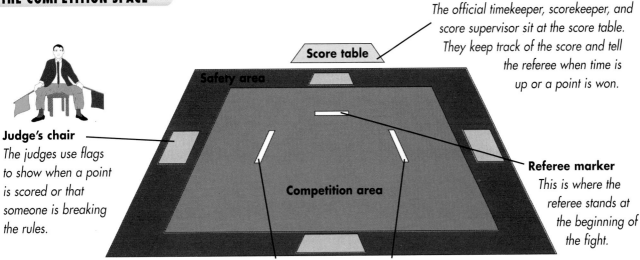

Score table
The official timekeeper, scorekeeper, and score supervisor sit at the score table. They keep track of the score and tell the referee when time is up or a point is won.

Score table

Safety area

Judge's chair
The judges use flags to show when a point is scored or that someone is breaking the rules.

Competition area

Referee marker
This is where the referee stands at the beginning of the fight.

Competitor markers
These two markers indicate the starting positions of the competitors. Each time the fight is stopped, competitors must return to their markers.

Points Scoring
Points are awarded for different moves. The scorekeeper signals the number of points with arm gestures.

Ippon
1 point

Nihon
2 points

Sanbon
3 points

WARMING UP & STRETCHING

Most karate classes start with a warm-up and stretching session. Stretches are often done at the end of the practice, as well. Stretching improves your flexibility, which helps build your technique and kicking ability.

KNEE BEND

Place your feet shoulder width apart.

Drop down by bending your knees, then rise up by straightening your legs.

KNEE LIFT

Stand with your feet shoulder width apart. Try to raise your knee to the same height as your shoulder.

UPPER BODY ROTATION

Stand with your feet shoulder width apart. Put your arms up in front of you with your elbows bent.

Rotate slowly side to side. Let your feet twist as you turn, raising the heel of your rear foot.

STOMACH CRUNCH

Lie on your back with your knees bent and feet flat on the floor. Place your hands on your thighs. Lift your upper body so that your hands reach over your knees. Keep your lower body still.

ARM STRETCH

Reach across your body with your arm. Use your other arm to stretch it further by pushing above the elbow.

HAMSTRING STRETCH

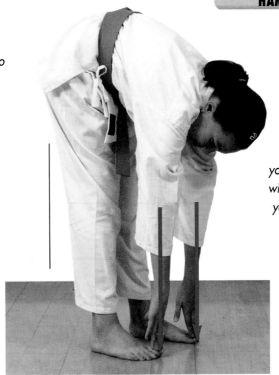

Stand with your feet shoulder width apart. Keep your legs straight as you touch your toes.

QUAD STRETCH

Stand on one leg and lift your other leg behind you. Keep your back straight. Make sure that your foot and knee are lifting straight back, not out to the side.

INSIDE LEG STRETCH

Don't bounce when stretching. Moving slowly into a static stretch works best.

Place your feet two shoulder widths apart. Keep your legs straight, bend from the waist, and reach to the floor.

STANCES

Stances are the foundation of karate technique. A stance is focused on how you position your legs and body. Your hand positions are free to change. Improving your stances not only makes your karate look better—it also helps keep your legs strong, which you need to perform quick and powerful techniques.

FRONT STANCE—ZENKUTSU DACHI

Bend your front knee, putting most of your weight on your front foot. Be sure that your front foot is pointing forward. Your rear foot should point forward at about 45 degrees.

Bend front knee

Rear foot at 45°

45°

Front foot pointing forward

BACK STANCE—KOKUTSU DACHI

Bend your back leg and put most of your weight on your back foot. Point your front foot forward and your back foot out to the side. Your hips should be turned so that they face to the side.

Weight on back foot

90°

Front foot pointing forward

HORSE-RIDING STANCE—*KIBA DACHI*

Bend both of your knees so that your weight is evenly distributed between either foot. Both feet point in the same direction.

Equal amount of weight on each leg

Feet parallel to each other

CAT STANCE—*NEKO ASHI DACHI*

Front leg slightly bent

Weight on back foot

Bend your back leg and put all of your weight on your back foot. Bend your front leg slightly.

FIGHTING POSTURE—*KAME*

Hands up in guard position

Head faces forward

Hips parallel to head

Front leg bent

Weight on toes

Put most of your weight on your front foot. Bend both knees. Put more weight on your toes than on your heels. Keep your hands up in guard position—they protect your body, but they are also ready to punch forward. Your hips are turned to the side, and your head faces forward.

PUNCHING

Punching is the most important technique in karate. Karate uses straight punches, which move directly from your hip to the target.

MAKING A FIST

You need to make a fist correctly so that you do not injure your hands when you punch. NEVER tuck your thumb inside your fingers.

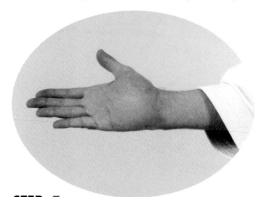

STEP 1

Open your hand.

STEP 2

Curl in your fingers tightly.

STEP 3

Put your thumb on top of your fingers, tucking it in as much as possible.

STANDING PUNCH—*CHOKU-ZUKI*

Practice your punches while standing still so that you can focus on good punching technique.

STEP 1

Start with your hands in fists, and hold them on your hips.

STEP 2

Push your fist forward, keeping your elbow behind the fist.

STEP 3

Straighten your arm and rotate your wrist inside. Make sure that you keep your wrist straight.

STEPPING PUNCH—OI-ZUKI

The stepping punch is used when you need to get close to your opponent quickly.

45°

STEP 1 *Start in front stance.*

Front hand back

Slide foot forward

STEP 2

Slide your rear foot forward so that your feet come together. Start pulling the front hand back, and begin pushing the punching hand forward.

STEP 3

Keep your foot moving so that you finish in front stance as you complete the punch.

JABBING PUNCH—KIZAMI-ZUKI

The jabbing punch allows you to keep your body protected while making a fast, head-level attack. Jabs can be used to test your opponent's defence, or to set up other, more powerful attacks.

Start in fighting posture, and punch using the leading hand. Turn your hips so that your chest turns to the side as you push your leading shoulder forward.

Push leading shoulder forward

Turn hips and shoulders

REVERSE PUNCH—GYAKU-ZUKI

The reverse punch is a stronger attack than the jab is, but be careful. Using this punch weakens your defenses and can expose you to a counterattack.

Start in the fighting posture, and punch using the rear hand. Turn your hips so that your chest faces forward as you push your rear shoulder forward.

Push shoulder forward

Rotate hips

KICKING

Kicks are the most impressive part of karate. They are also some of the most difficult moves to master. Kicks require not only great skill, timing, and agility, but also strength and flexibility. When sparring, kicks are slower than punchesare and they can briefly leave you stuck in one place. However, using your feet to attack leaves your hands free to defend—kicks are your most powerful attack.

FRONT KICK—MAE GERI

The front kick is a very fast kick. It is usually done with a snapping motion so that you hit your opponent with the ball of the foot. Sometimes a thrusting motion is used to push the opponent back.

Arms out to the side

STEP 1

Start in front stance with your arms out to the side. Keep your hands in this position throughout the kick.

45°

Raise knee

STEP 2

Lift your knee, ready to kick. The higher you lift your knee, the higher you can kick.

Kick with ball of foot

Hips move forward

STEP 3

Extend your bent knee, kicking forward. Point the foot forward, but pull your toes back so that you make contact using the ball of your foot.

Do not drop knee

Make sure that you have warmed up your leg muscles before trying any high kicks.

STEP 4

Immediately snap your foot back. Don't let your knee drop down yet.

STEP 5

Land in front stance.

SIDE-THRUSTING KICK — *YOKO KEKOMI*

This is a thrusting kick, so it can be used to stop or push your opponent. In self-defence situations, it can be a very powerful attack to the side or back of an opponent's knee.

Feet parallel

STEP 1
Start in horse-riding stance. Put your hands up as a fighting guard. Point them in the direction tha you are facing.

Step forward

Knees are bent

STEP 2
Step your rear foot across and in front of the other foot. Keep your weight low and your knees bent.

Raise knee

STEP 3
Lift your knee, ready to kick. If you lift your leg high, you can kick high.

Heel higher than toes

Spin on back foot

STEP 4
Thrust your foot out. Turn your hips away from the kick so that your foot turns sideways and your heel is slightly higher than your toes.

Spin on back foot

STEP 5
Pull your knee back, as in Step 3.

STEP 6
Step down into horse-riding stance.

SIDE-RISING KICK—*YOKO KEAGE*

This side kick is similar to the side-thrusting kick, but it is faster and more direct. It uses a quick push-pull hip action to whip your foot out and then back.

Side view

Knee points in direction of kick

Foot rests on knee

Feet parallel

STEP 1
Start in horse-riding stance.

Step forward

Knees are bent

STEP 2
Step your rear foot across and in front of the other foot. Keep your weight low and your knees bent.

STEP 3
Lift the knee of your front leg so that the kicking foot rests on your other knee. Point the kicking knee in the direction that you want to kick.

Hips move forward

Spin on back foot

STEP 4
Lift your knee higher, and push your hips toward the target as you straighten your leg.

Spin on back foot

STEP 5
Immediately snap the foot back to your knee.

STEP 6
Step down into horse-riding stance.

The roundhouse kick—also known as the round or turning kick—is very popular in karate tournaments. It is the most likely kick to score points. Traditionally, it hits with the ball of the foot. In tournaments, you must make safe contact, so hit with the top surface of the foot instead.

STEP 1
Start in fighting stance.

45°

Raise kicking foot almost as high as knee

Side view

STEP 2
Lift your back leg. Angle your kicking leg so that your foot is almost as high as your knee.

STEP 3
Rotate your hips.

Spin on foot

STEP 4
Kick by letting your foot flick forward. Don't let your support foot stick to the ground or you won't be able to turn.

STEP 5
Snap the kicking foot back.

Spin on foot

STEP 6
Step down into fighting stance.

Front view

TOP TIP
Improving flexibility is the key to improving your kicks. By doing 20 minutes of stretching each day, you will quickly increase how high you can kick.

BACK KICK—USHIRO GERI

This powerful kick uses the heel to strike with a thrusting action.

STEP 1
Start in fighting stance.

Most of weight on front foot

Weight on toes

Rotate hips

Bring knee of back leg forward and up

Supporting leg is slightly bent

Spin on foot

STEP 2
Rotate on the spot, and lift your back foot. Bring your back leg forward, and raise the foot close to the knee of your support leg.

Hips should turn down

Make contact using heel

Toes of kicking foot point toward ground

Support leg slightly bent

Support foot is able to move

STEP 3
Thrust your foot backward in a straight line. Be sure that your kicking leg moves close by your support leg. As you kick, throw your arms in the direction of the kick.

Kicking foot returns to support knee

STEP 4
Pull your foot straight back. Make sure that it moves in a straight line and that your foot finishes on your support knee.

HOOK KICK—URA MAWASHI GERI

The hook kick is also known as a "reverse-roundhouse kick". It starts as a slightly off-target thrust kick, but then you hook your leg in to hit with your heel. To make this kick safer in a tournament, you should strike with the base of your foot instead.

Hands up in guard

Weight on toes

STEP 1
Start in fighting stance with your hands up as a defensive guard.

Lift front knee

STEP 2
Lift your front knee, and keep your hands in the guard position.

Twist hips

STEP 3
Twist your hip and kick—hook your leg in to strike with your heel. To increase the power of your hook, bend your knee.

STEP 4
Pull your leg back, and don't let your knee drop. Your leg should come back along the path that you used for the kick.

Don't let knee drop

STEP 5
Step back down into fighting posture.

BLOCKING

In karate, the key to defending yourself is blocking. Blocks are used to deflect incoming attacks, but these same techniques can be used to attack an opponent. You can block with either hand, depending on where you expect an attack to come from.

DOWNWARD BLOCK—*GEDAN BARAI*

STEP 1

Prepare for the block by crossing your arms. Lift your blocking arm so that it is beside your ear.

Blocking arm by ear

Leading arm straight

Weight on back foot.

STEP 2

Step forward into a front stance, and block down. Pull your other fist up to your hip. The blocking arm should twist at the end so that your palm faces down.

Swing blocking arm forward and down

Bring other hand back to hip

Rotate fist

Back leg is straight

Step forward with front leg

TOP TIP
Use this checklist to improve your downward block.

- **The fist of your blocking hand should finish just above your front knee.**
- **Your blocking arm should finish straight.**
- **Make sure that your opposite fist is pulled back to your hip.**
- **Your body should be turned to the side so that you are hiding behind your blocking arm.**

Non-blocking hand is open

Extend arm above head

Blocking hand pulls to hip

Legs are slightly bent.

Most of weight on back foot

STEP 1
Prepare for the block by pulling the blocking hand to your hip and reaching with the opposite hand.

Pull non-blocking arm back to support blocking arm

Move blocking arm forward and up

STEP 2
Start blocking as if punching up from the hip, and then move in front of your face. At the same time, pull back your other hand so that your arms cross.

Swing blocking hand up in front of forehead

Pull non-blocking hand back to hip

Most of weight on front foot

Back leg is straight

STEP 3
Step forward into a front stance, and complete the block by pushing the elbow up. Pull your other fist to your hip.

TOP TIP
Use this checklist to improve your rising block.

- The forearm of your blocking hand should finish just in front of your forehead.
- Your blocking arm should finish bent.
- Make sure that your opposite fist is pulled back to your hip.
- Your body should be turned to the side so that your blocking arm is pushed forward.

Pull blocking arm back behind head

Blocking hand in fist

STEP 1
Get ready by pulling the blocking hand behind your head. Reach forward with your other hand.

Reach straight forward with non-blocking hand

Even when your body rotates back, keep your head facing forward—never take your eyes off of your opponent.

Weight on back foot

Bring blocking arm forward

Rotate body

Pull hand back to hip, palm up

STEP 2
Step forward into a front stance. Complete the block by rotating your body and swinging your blocking arm around. Pull your other hand to your hip. Rotate the blocking wrist so that your palm faces toward you.

Back leg straight

Most of weight on front foot

INSIDE BLOCK—UCHI UKE

Open non-blocking hand and reach forward

Blocking hand moves back

STEP 1
Prepare for the block by moving your blocking hand across your body and reaching with the opposite hand.

Standing on toes of front foot

Most of weight on back foot

Arm comes forward in smooth movement

Hand pulls back to hip

Back leg straight

Most of weight on front foot

STEP 2
Step forward into a front stance, and complete the block. Pull back the opposite hand to your hip. Twist the blocking wrist so that your palm faces toward you.

TOP TIP
Use this checklist to improve your inside and outside blocks.

• The fist of your blocking hand should finish at the same height as your shoulder.
• Your blocking arm should finish bent 90 degrees.
• Make sure that your opposite fist is pulled back to your hip.
• Your body should be turned to the side so that you are hiding behind your blocking arm.

KNIFE-HAND BLOCK—*UCHI UKE*

Both hands open

Front leg straight

STEP 1
Get ready by opening both hands and crossing your arms. Lift your blocking arm so that it is beside your ear.

Palm faces outward

Leg bent

STEP 2
Step backward into a back stance. Bring your blocking hand forward with your elbow bent and your palm facing outward. Pull your other hand back to the center of your body.

Step back

Weight on back foot

TOP TIP
Use this checklist to improve your knife-hand block.

- Hit with the fleshy part of the hand.
- Keep your fingers together.
- Keep your wrist straight.
- Don't let your elbows stick out. Keep them tucked close to the center of your body.

STEP 1
Prepare by opening both hands. Cross your arms at the wrists in front of your stomach.

Cross arms at wrists

Both hands open

Front heel raised

Back leg bent

Weight on back foot

In most blocks, you turn your hips so that your body faces sideways. In the cross block, you face forward because you are using both hands to block.

Hands move up together

Back leg straight

Weight moves to front foot

STEP 2
Step forward, and thrust both hands out and up above your head.

TOP TIP
Use this checklist to improve your cross block.

- **Keep your fingers together.**
- **Keep your wrists straight.**
- **Make sure that you push the block high enough to send the attack over your head.**

FOOTWORK DRILLS

*G*ood footwork is key to winning sparring matches. If you are light on your feet and move quickly, then you can more easily evade attacks or hit your opponent. The key to fast footwork is to keep your weight on the balls of your feet and to keep your legs bent. This is hard work that requires strong muscles and practice.

SLIDING JAB

This is a quick attack that can be used to test your opponent's defences or as an opening move in a combination. It does not reach as far as a stepping punch does, but it is faster.

STEP 1

Start in fighting posture with your weight on your front leg.

STEP 2

Slightly lift your front foot, and push with your back leg. This will propel you forward. As you move forward, punch with your front hand. Don't shift your weight to your back leg, or you won't move as quickly.

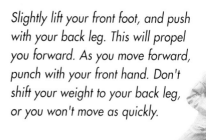

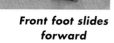

Front foot slides forward

Back leg follows

STEP 3

As your weight comes down on your front foot, drag your rear leg and punching arm in. Finish in fighting stance, ready for your next move.

SLIDING CROSS

This is not as fast as the sliding jab is, but it can penetrate your opponent's defences if it is done right. Use a strong hip motion to drive the punch forward.

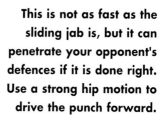

Back leg straight

STEP 1

Start in fighting posture with your weight on your front leg.

STEP 2

Pick up your front foot slightly, and push with your back leg. As you move forward, rotate your hips so that your chest faces forward. Punch with your rear hand to stomach level.

Rear hand punches

STEP 3

As your weight comes down on your front foot, drag your rear leg and punching arm in. Finish in fighting stance, ready for your next move.

Use the switch to avoid an attack and then counterattack immediately. This takes practice to learn. You must move back far enough to avoid the attack. If you move back too far, you will not reach your opponent with the counterattack.

Weight on front leg

STEP 2

Slide your front leg back toward your other leg while blocking down with your front hand. Try not to shift too much weight to your back leg.

STEP 1

Start in fighting posture with your weight on your front leg.

STEP 3

Step forward with your other leg, and punch to either head or stomach level.

With the correct footwork, you can kick much faster. This footwork can be used with any of the kicks to produce a rapid attack. The key is to use your front leg to do the kick, and skip in quickly to close the distance.

Weight on front leg

Rotate hips

Back leg slides back

STEP 1

Start in fighting posture.

STEP 2

Skip in with your back leg and immediately lift your front knee. Twist your hip to produce a roundhouse kick.

STEP 3

Slide your support leg back, and immediately bring your front foot down to take its place.

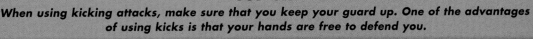

TOP TIP
When using kicking attacks, make sure that you keep your guard up. One of the advantages of using kicks is that your hands are free to defend you.

BASIC SPARRING DRILLS

Sparring drills are used to practice attacking and defending with a partner. All karate techniques must be controlled—this means stopping your attacks just before you actually hit your partner. Control is especially important when performing a head-level attack.

DEFENCE AGAINST HEAD-LEVEL PUNCH

Defender

Opponent

Weight on front foot

STEP 1

Face your opponent in fighting stance.

Push blocking arm up

Rotate body

Slide back with both feet

STEP 2

As your opponent punches, slide back, and deflect the punch above your head with a rising block. Twist your body so that your blocking arm is pushed forward toward the attack. Your opposite arm is pulled back, ready for your counter attack.

Pull blocking arm back to hip

Rotate hips

Reverse punch

STEP 3

Punch with your non-blocking hand. Rotate your body so that your arm is pushed forward and can reach your opponent. This is called a "reverse punch".

Defender

Opponent

Weight on toes

DEFENCE AGAINST MIDDLE-LEVEL PUNCH

STEP 1

Face your opponent in fighting stance.

Swing blocking arm in

Pull arm back

Twist body

Slide back

STEP 2

As your opponent punches, slide back and deflect the punch to the side with an outside block. Twist your body to add extra power to the block. Your opposite arm should be pulled back, ready for your counterattack. Your body should be turned to the side so that it is protected behind your blocking arm.

Pull blocking arm back to hip

Rotate hips

Punch to stomach

STEP 3

Rotate your body as you reverse punch so that your punching arm is pushed forward far enough to reach your opponent.

TOP TIP
Don't overreach by leaning so that your head comes forward when you punch. If you are too far away, then you need to use your legs to get closer.

DEFENCE AGAINST FRONT KICK

Defender

Opponent

STEP 1

Face your opponent in fighting stance.

Weight on front foot

Block with front arm

Back foot slides to side

STEP 2

As your opponent kicks, slide away from the attack to the side. Hit the inside of the leg with a downward block. Don't try to push away the kick—you will not be able to stop this strong attack. Your body movement is your main defence. Aim for your block to contact with the side or underside of the kicking leg.

Blocking arm to hip

Rotate hips

Punch with non-blocking arm

Slide foot forward if necessary

STEP 3

Reverse punch to the stomach. Remember to turn your hips forward to reach your opponent. If you need to reach farther, slide your foot forward.

DEFENCE AGAINST SIDE KICK

Defender

Opponent

Weight on toes, ready to move

STEP 1

Face your opponent in fighting stance.

Outside block to opponent's leg

Slide to the side

STEP 2

As your opponent kicks, slide to the side, and hit the back of the leg with an outside block. However, do not try to reach the kick if it is very low or off target—you will lose your balance.

Punch to stomach

Blocking hand to hip

STEP 3

Counterattack with a reverse punch to the stomach. If your block pushed your opponent off-balance, you can counter attack with a reverse punch aimed at his or her back.

TOP TIP

When blocking a kick, you must use body motion to evade the kick. If you try to block directly, you could bruise your arm.

DEFENCE AGAINST ROUNDHOUSE KICK

Defender

Opponent

Weight on front foot

STEP 1

Face your opponent in fighting stance.

STEP 2

As your opponent kicks, slide away from the kick, and deflect the leg with an inside block. Rotate your body, and swing your blocking arm around. Be sure that you keep your blocking arm firm to stop this kick.

Keep blocking arm firm

Back foot slides to side

Swing body around

Twist hips

Reverse punch to stomach

Slide foot forward if necessary

STEP 3

As your opponent steps forward after the kick, counterattack with a reverse punch at the stomach.

Defender

Opponent

Weight on toes, not heels

STEP 1

Face your opponent in fighting stance.

Bring blocking arm forward to opponent's leg

STEP 2

This kick is hard to stop but easy to deflect. As your opponent kicks, slide to the side, and deflect the leg with an outside block. As long as you stay off the line of attack, you can practice moving closer to your opponent to improve your counterattack.

Rotate body

Evade by sliding back foot sideways

Reverse punch to back or ribs

Rotate at hips

STEP 3

Your opponent will step forward and past you after the kick. You are now at his or her side—this is called a "flanking position". Counterattack with a reverse punch to the back or the ribs.

ADVANCED SPARRING DRILLS

Putting moves together in attacking combinations can help you score points in a match. Practice these set pieces often until they feel natural. This will give you the best chance of remembering them when you need to use them.

ROUNDHOUSE-KICK COMBINATION

A good way to score with a roundhouse kick is to force your opponent to bring his or her hands up to protect his or her head. This move exposes his or her body to your kick.

STEP 1

Face your opponent in fighting stance.

STEP 2

Slide your front foot forward while throwing a jab to the head. This attack draws your opponent's guard up.

STEP 3

Push your opposite hip forward, and throw a reverse punch to the head—this again forces your opponent to block.

STEP 4

Continue the forward motion of your hip. Lift your right knee and perform a roundhouse kick to the unprotected body.

FOOT-SWEEP COMBINATION

A foot sweep is a great way to unbalance your opponent, but it won't work if your opponent's weight is on the front foot. This combination's head attacks make your opponent move backward and take weight off the front foot. Now your opponent is open to a foot sweep.

Opponent   **Attacker**

Twist your body

Slide foot

Punch to the head

Twist at hips

Weight moves to back foot

STEP 1

Start in a fighting stance. Slide your front foot forward, and jab to the head. Improve your reach by twisting your body to the side so that your punching arm is pushed forward.

STEP 2

Twist your body in the opposite direction, and reverse punch to the head. This punch must be aimed at the head to unbalance your opponent. Your opponent's weight will move to his or her back leg.

Opponent is knocked off balance

Hips continue to rotate

Swing back foot behind opponent's foot

Reverse punch

Hand back to hip

Twist feet

Move weight to front foot

STEP 3

Continue the forward motion of your hip. Swing your back leg around to sweep your opponent's front foot.

STEP 4

In tournaments, a sweep is not considered a finishing move. To complete your combination, strike your unbalanced opponent with a reverse punch.

SELF-DEFENCE

*K*arate is an effective form of self-defence. When practicing self-defence techniques with your partner, be careful not to injure anyone.

ESCAPE FROM A WRIST GRAB

THE HOLD

Opponent   **Defender**

Opponent grabs wrist

STEP 1

This move can be used when your opponent tries to grab your wrist.

Twist shoulders and hips

Bring arm across body

Twist foot 90 degrees

STEP 2

Step out to the side, and swing your arm out the same way. Make sure that you turn your whole body to the side, and bend your front leg.

Take hold of wrist and elbow

Push arm forward

Rotate hips

STEP 3

Keep your hand moving in a big circle. Your other hand joins in this movement and pushes on your opponent's elbow. Use your whole body to drive this motion by rotating your hips.

Put weight on elbow

STEP 4

Circle your hand down, grasp your opponent's wrist, and press down with your other hand on the elbow. Put your body weight behind this movement by bending your front knee and dropping down.

Opponent

Defender

Opponent uses bear hug

STEP 1

Use this move if your opponent grabs you from behind.

Move head back

STEP 2

Rock backward, and push your head into your opponent's face. This acts as a distraction and may weaken the hold on you.

STEP 3

Rock forward again. and step out to the side. Bend your knee so that you drop your weight. At the same time, swing your arm back and elbow your opponent in the stomach.

Strike with elbow

Step sideways

Take hold of opponent's arm

STEP 4

Grab your opponent's arm with both hands.

Drop weight to opposite foot

Hold on tight, and turn your body

STEP 5

Hold tightly. Partly lift your opponent, as if you are lifting a heavy backpack onto your shoulder. Turn your body, and drop your weight onto the opposite foot, throwing your opponent over you.

DEFENCE AGAINST DOWN SWING

If someone attacks with a weapon, you must avoid contact with the weapon by blocking the attack on your opponent's arm.

Defender   **Opponent**

STEP 1

Your opponent raises his or her hand and prepares to attack.

Raise arms to block

STEP 2

Block the downward motion by crossing your arms, and stopping your opponent's forearm.

Step forward

Grab wrist   **Push down on elbow**

STEP 3

Grab the opponent's wrist with your right hand, while pressing on the elbow with your left hand. Step past your opponent and lock his or her arm straight by placing pressure on the elbow.

Step forward   **Continue to apply pressure**

STEP 4

Step in toward your opponent's elbow to keep it locked straight. Bend your front knee, and drop your weight down on the arm to bring him or her to the ground. This allows you to restrain him or her or to escape.

Opponent · **Strike with palm** · **Defender** · **Block**

A swinging punch is a common attack by untrained fighters. It is a powerful attack but is easy to defend.

STEP 1

Your opponent swings a hooking punch. Deflect the punch with an inside block. At the same time, counterattack by striking your palm to the attacker's chin.

Push under chin · **Hook your foot behind opponent's**

STEP 2

Step forward, and hook your foot in behind your opponent's front leg so that you finish in close to him or her. Push under his or her chin so that he or she lean back.

Step back with front leg · **Grab and pull wrist**

Do not attempt throwing techniques unless your partner knows how to fall safely. Use soft crash mats to help break the fall.

STEP 3

Grab your opponent's wrist with your left hand. Thrust your front leg back so that it lifts your opponent's front leg and trips him or her. At the same time, push down on your opponent's upper body with your right hand, and pull the wrist with your left hand.

KARATE TOURNAMENTS

The World Karate Federation (WKF) is the recognized international sport federation for karate. It represents the agreed rules taken from the various styles of karate around the world.

There are five main types of karate events:

- Individual kata
- Team kata
- Individual kumite (sparring)
- Team kumite (sparring)
- Kumite rules (sparring)

SCORING POINTS

In a kumite match, the competitors score points using effective, but controlled, techniques. Successful attacks score one, two, or three points based on difficulty of the move. The match finishes when a competitor has scored eight or more points, or the time limit for the match is reached.

Attacks are limited to the following areas:

- Head
- Face
- Neck
- Abdomen
- Chest
- Back
- Side

THREE POINTS

The most difficult attacks score three points—or *sanbon* in Japanese.

Punches on ground:
This involves throwing or sweeping the opponent to the mat, followed by a scoring technique like a punch.

Head-level kicks:
The roundhouse kick is the most common head-level kick in karate matches.

Punches on the back:
These include punches to the back of the head and neck.

These moves score two points, which translates into Japanese as *nihon.*

Stomach-level kicks:
Front kicks and side-thrusting kicks can be used, but the roundhouse kick is the most common kick in matches.

Combination hand techniques:
An example of this combination would be a jab to the head, followed by a reverse punch to the body.

Sweeps:
Unbalancing the opponent—for example, with a foot sweep—and scoring with an attack such as a reverse punch.

The quickest and easiest attacks score only one point, which is *ippon* in Japanese.

Punches:
For example, a jabbing punch to the head.

Backfist strikes:
This attack involves snapping the arm forward from the elbow, to strike with the back of the fist.

These techniques are too dangerous to use in a karate tournament:

Knee strikes
Elbow strikes
Head butts
Open-handed attacks to the face
Any attack that makes contact with the throat

DIET & MENTAL ATTITUDE

*E*ating healthy for both training and competitions can give you the edge. A good diet improves your performance by making sure that you always have plenty of energy.

DIET

This is the recommended intake for the balanced and healthy diet that is essential to karate experts.

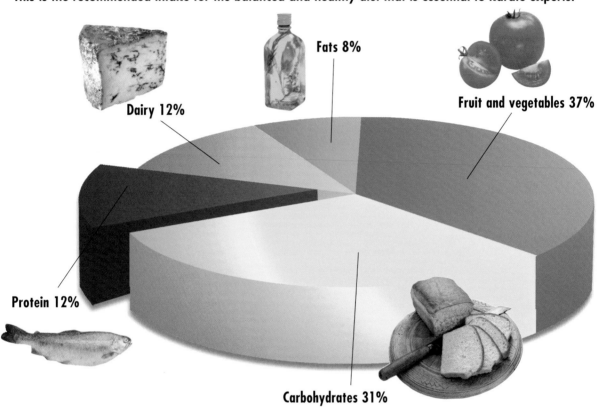

Fats 8%

Dairy 12%

Fruit and vegetables 37%

Protein 12%

Carbohydrates 31%

BEFORE TRAINING

Before training, you should eat carbohydrates, because they are good energy foods.

Karate-training sessions normally last one to two hours. Eat a snack within an hour before exercise to keep yourself from feeling hungry. Karate competitions are usually all-day events with many breaks. Bring carbohydrate snacks like bananas and sandwiches to eat during breaks.

DURING TRAINING

Karate can be hot work, and it's important to stay hydrated.

It is a good idea to drink before beginning any exercise. Then drink regularly after the first 30 minutes of exercise. Water is great for short practices. Sports drinks are better for longer training sessions.

MENTAL ATTITUDE

Physical training is only part of karate—your mental attitude is just as important. Training to become a black belt and for competitions requires patience and dedication. Karate performances can be determined by how confident you look.

AWARENESS

Be aware of your surroundings and your opponent. The Japanese call this "zanshin". You must be aware of any possible attack in order to defend yourself.

OPEN MIND

Being aware of a coming attack is not enough. You must also be in the proper state of mind to react. Your mind must be open to any possibility. The Japanese call this "mushin". If you only plan around one type of attack, then you will be unable to act quickly to other attacks. Fear blocks an open, reactive mind. Through karate training, you can overcome your fears and learn to react quickly.

STRONG SPIRIT

A strong spirit and positive attitude can help you overcome setbacks and challenges. One method used by a sensei to build spirit is to use a martial shout called a "kiai". Voicing a strong "kiai!" when you attack builds your courage. This loud call can also intimidate your opponent.

PERSEVERANCE

Training to become a black belt can take anywhere between three and five years. A typical student trains two to three times a week to reach this level. Becoming a skilled martial artist takes many years of training and commitment. You must stay motivated and focused to achieve this goal. Karate training is mostly about repeating moves until they become natural reactions.

COURTESY AND RESPECT

You should be polite to everyone, including your opponents. If you do not have respect for your opponents' abilities, then you are in danger of underestimating them.

DON'T PANIC!

Stay calm and focused. Do not lose your temper—karate requires focused attacks, not anger. People who get angry act foolishly, and they are easily defeated.

HOW THE EXPERTS DO IT

Karate tournaments are very popular among young people participating in karate. They are particularly popular with university students.

MONEY

There is little money to be made from winning karate tournaments—most competitions offer no prize money at all.

Winners of big karate tournaments can build their fame and use this toward other careers. For example, movie stars like Cynthia Rothrock and Jean-Claude Van Damme were successful karate competitors before they starred in martial-arts movies. However, most people who go on to become karate professionals run their own clubs or karate associations.

Japanese karate champion Yuka Sato poses with a bouquet and mascot at the Olympics.

Wayne Otto is a karate champion from the United Kingdom.

COMPETITIONS

There are many types of karate competitions.

The smallest ones are internal club competitions, which only take one or two hours. The largest competitions are international tournaments like the Shoto World Cup, which takes three days. There are many regional and national tournaments that usually take one day.

A typical tournament day might look like this:

7:00   *Wake up*

7:30   *Eat high-energy breakfast*

8:00   *Get on bus and travel to venue*

9:15   *Arrive at venue and register*

9:30   *Get changed*

9:45   *Team warm-up and pep talk*

10:00 *Tournament starts. Competitors wait for their events in preliminary rounds.*

4:00   *Final rounds*

5:00   *Medal awards ceremony*

6:00   *Tournament finishes. Return to bus, and head home.*

7:30   *Team dinner. Reflect together on successes and failures of the day.*

Your actual matches may only last one or two minutes each, which will mean a lot of sitting around and waiting. During this time, make sure that you stay warm and have snacks on hand to keep energized. It can be useful to watch other competitors to analyze their strengths and weaknesses—you might face them in a later round.

Two karate experts face off in a championship match.

GLOSSARY

COUNTER – *An attack used in response to or to block an opponent's attack.*

CRASH MAT – *A thick pad placed on the floor to protect someone falling on the ground.*

DAN – *The skill level of someone who has reached black belt.*

DOJO – *Karate training hall. This literally means "place of the way".*

EVADE – *To dodge an attack.*

FIGHTING POSTURE – *An informal fighting stance with the arms ready to attack or defend and the legs bent to allow for rapid movement.*

FOCUS PAD – *A small pad for practising the accuracy of strikes.*

FRONT STANCE – *A formal posture often used for lunge attacks with most of the weight on the front knee.*

GI – *Traditional karate uniform.*

HAMSTRING – *A tendon in the back of the knee.*

JAB – *A fast punch using the leading hand.*

KATA – *Traditional forms usually consisting of between 20 and 110 choreographed moves, as if fighting a series of imaginary opponents.*

KYU – *A grade below black belt. The highest of these grades is 1st kyu, and the lowest is usually 10th kyu (white belt).*

QUAD – *This is short for quadricep, a muscle on the front of the thigh.*

SENSEI – *Karate instructor.*

SPAR – *To fight without putting your full strength into your attacks.*

SWEEP – *A leg technique used to knock an opponent's foot or lower leg in order to unbalance him or her.*

THROW – *A grappling move where an opponent is unbalanced and is forced to fall to the ground.*

INDEX

Printed in the USA